FRANCE

Jillian Powell
with photographs by Julia Davey

The Bookwright Press
New York • 1991

Our Country

Australia
Canada
China
France
India
Italy
Japan
New Zealand
Spain
The United Kingdom
West Germany

Cover *People strolling in a Paris street near the famous Arc de Triomphe.*

First published in the
United States in 1991 by
The Bookwright Press
387 Park Avenue South
New York, NY 10016

First published in 1990 by
Wayland (Publishers) Ltd
61 Western Road, Hove
East Sussex BN3 1JD, England

© Copyright 1990 Wayland (Publishers) Ltd

Library of Congress Cataloging-in-Publication Data

Powell, Jillian.
  France / Jillian Powell.
    p. cm. — (Our country)
  Includes bibliographical references and index.
  Summary: An introduction to France with brief surveys of the
weather, work, education, religion, and culture, accompanied by
interviews with children on each subject.
  ISBN 0–531–18372–6
  1. France — Social life and customs — 20th century — Juvenile
literature. [1. France.] I. Title. II. Series: Our country (New
York, N.Y.)
DC33.7.P68 1991
944.08—dc20   90—37568
                                                  CIP
                                                   AC

Typeset by Nicola Taylor, Wayland
Printed in Italy by G. Canale & C.S.p.A. Turin

All words printed in **bold** are explained in the glossary on page 30.

Contents

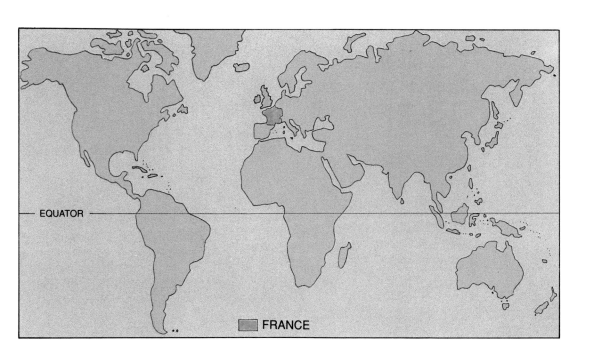

EQUATOR

FRANCE

We live in France

France is a large country at the western end of Europe. To the east it has borders with five other countries. France has a long coastline, with sandy beaches and rocky cliffs. To the south is the Mediterranean Sea. The island of Corsica is part of France.

France has beautiful rivers, forests and mountains, as well as rich farmland. There are big cities like Paris and Lyons, old market towns and pretty villages.

The French are famous for their beautiful buildings and works of art, fashions, perfumes, cooking, wines and cheeses.

In this book, twelve children living in different parts of the country talk about their lives.

Grapes are grown in many parts of France for making wine. These vineyards are in Alsace, in eastern France.

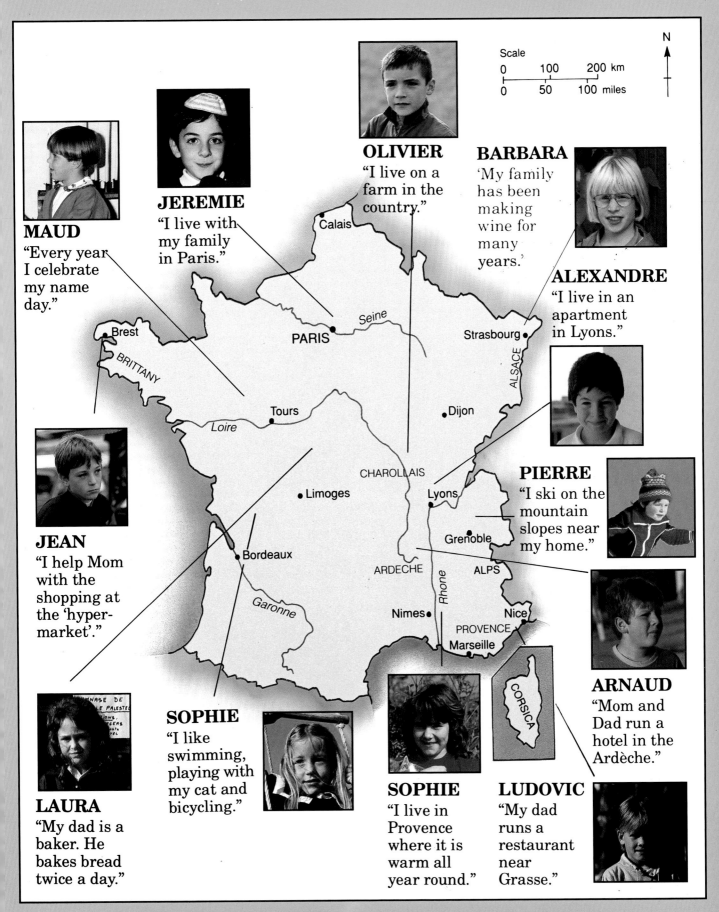

MAUD
"Every year I celebrate my name day."

JEREMIE
"I live with my family in Paris."

OLIVIER
"I live on a farm in the country."

BARBARA
'My family has been making wine for many years.'

ALEXANDRE
"I live in an apartment in Lyons."

JEAN
"I help Mom with the shopping at the 'hyper-market'."

PIERRE
"I ski on the mountain slopes near my home."

ARNAUD
"Mom and Dad run a hotel in the Ardèche."

SOPHIE
"I like swimming, playing with my cat and bicycling."

LAURA
"My dad is a baker. He bakes bread twice a day."

SOPHIE
"I live in Provence where it is warm all year round."

LUDOVIC
"My dad runs a restaurant near Grasse."

Scale
0   100   200 km
0   50   100 miles

N

Calais
Seine
PARIS
Brest
BRITTANY
Strasbourg
ALSACE
Tours
Loire
Dijon
CHAROLLAIS
Limoges
Lyons
Bordeaux
Grenoble
ARDECHE
ALPS
Garonne
Rhone
Nimes
Nice
PROVENCE
Marseille
CORSICA

5

The weather

Because France is a large country, the weather is not the same everywhere. In the north it can be wet and cold. In the south (called The Midi) the weather is much warmer, with mild winters and hot, dry summers.

Along the Mediterranean coast, it is often very dry in the summer and forest fires can be a danger. In the winter a cold, north wind called the mistral blows down the valley of the Rhône River.

Moist winds from the Atlantic Ocean bring plenty of rain to the north and west coasts. These **regions** have cool summers and mild winters. Inland, in the east, it is much drier, with cold winters and hot summers.

Many people enjoy the warm climate and sunshine of the south.

In the mountain regions there is lots of snow in the winter, and the mountain tops may be snow-covered all through the year.

"I like playing outdoors in the sun."

"My name is Sophie. I live in Provence, in the south of France. It is warm all year round here. In the winter, we don't often have snow, but sometimes a cold wind blows. I like summer best because I like playing outdoors in the sun. Here I am with my new kitten."

"Skiing is my favorite sport."

"My name is Pierre. I live in the Alps, near Grenoble. We often have lots of snow in the winter and it can be very cold. I love it when it snows because then I can go skiing on the mountain slopes near my home. I learned to ski when I was quite small. It is my favorite sport, especially when the snow is crisp and the sun is shining."

Farming

France has a lot of rich farmland. Most of the land is used for growing cereal crops, fruit and vegetables, **pastures** for sheep and cattle, and trees for lumber.

Because the weather and soil are not the same all over France, there are many different types of farms.

Milk, cheese and butter are produced by the dairy farmers of the north, where cattle graze the rich pastureland. On the low-lying, chalky plains of the countryside around Paris, huge fields of wheat, barley and corn are grown. Farther south, the warm sun ripens fruit such as melons, peaches and cherries, and fields of

A farmer plowing a field for cereal crops in the Bordeaux region of France.

8

"My family makes wine."

"My name is Barbara. My family has been making wine for many years. Dad and Grandpa look after the grapes growing in our **vineyard**, and every year they make 70,000 bottles of wine. Most of the grapes are harvested in September or October, but some are left on the vine to make a special strong, sweet wine. Here I am helping Grandpa pick grapes."

"We raise cattle for beef."

"I am Olivier, and I live on a farm in the Charollais region of France. We raise Charollais cattle for beef and we also grow wheat and corn. In the summer, the cattle graze in the fields. In the winter, they are kept in stables. We keep goats too, and my aunts make butter, cream and cheese from the goats' milk."

sunflowers are grown for oil and margarine. Cattle, sheep and goats provide meat and milk, and many different cheeses are made.

Industry and jobs

France has many industries. These include the production of iron and steel, machinery, aircraft, cars and chemicals. France's car industry is one of the biggest in the world.

Tourism is another important industry. Every year thousands of people visit Paris, the Mediterranean coast and other popular areas. In the winter, skiers flock to the snow-covered slopes of the Alps.

France's wine, perfume and fashion industries are world famous. Grapes are grown for wines in most regions of France. Fields of lavender are grown in the south. The oils from lavender and other plants are

France has many nuclear power stations like this one in the Rhône valley.

used for making perfume. The fashion industry is centered in Paris, where the big **fashion shows** are held.

"Dad bakes bread and cakes and Mom sells them."

"My name is Laura. My father is a baker and Mom sells the bread and cakes he makes in our bakery shop. There are lots of small shops like ours in France, run as family businesses. Dad is showing me how he mixes the dough for the bread."

"People come to enjoy the sun and the scenery."

"My name is Arnaud. Mom and Dad run a hotel in the Ardèche. Vacationers come from all over Europe, as well as from other parts of France, to stay at our hotel. They come to enjoy the sun, the beautiful scenery and sports like canoeing, horseback riding and bicycling."

Schools

Many children start nursery school when they are three years old. At the age of six they go to elementary school, where they will learn reading, writing and arithmetic. Children spend five years at elementary school, before moving on to high school, or to a trade or technical school.

Most schools in France are run by the government. There are also a number of private schools, many of them run by the Roman Catholic Church.

An arithmetic class at an elementary school.

"I have just started to learn English."

"I am Arnaud. I go to the village school. It's a private school run by the Roman Catholic Church. I have just started to learn English. We play games on the playground. I am running for the ball but I am way at the back. Can you see me?"

"I go to a state elementary school in Lyons."

"My name is Alexandre, and I live in Lyons. I go to a state elementary school near my home. My favorite classes are geography and science. Here I am at home doing my science homework."

School usually begins at 8:30 in the morning and lasts until 4:00 in the afternoon. Some children go home for lunch, others eat in the school cafeteria. After school there is homework for older children. There may be classes on Saturday mornings too, but Wednesdays are usually free.

Religion

The main religion in France is Roman Catholicism, which is a branch of **Christianity**. Children take their first **communion** at about seven years old and they receive **confirmation** a few years later.

Many people who live in France today follow other religions. In the past, France had **colonies** in different parts of the world. A lot of people came originally from these colonies to live and work in France. Many of them come from North Africa, where most people follow the religion of **Islam**. There are also many French people

France has many beautiful churches. This one is Sacré Coeur, in Paris.

who practice the Jewish religion.

Because there are so many people from different cultural backgrounds and with different religions, France is now a **multicultural** society.

"Every year I celebrate my name day."

"My name is Maud. My family is Roman Catholic, and we go to church every Sunday. Here I am lighting a candle in our church. Every year I celebrate my name day. I am named after Ste. Matilda, so Mom tells me stories about her, and I have a cake and a little present. It's almost like a second birthday!"

"I listen to stories of the Jewish prophets."

"My name is Jeremie, and I am Jewish. I live in Paris and once a week after school I go to religious classes. I listen to stories of the Jewish prophets and learn to read and write the **Hebrew script**."

Festivals

The festival of **Mardi Gras** *is celebrated in Nice with colorful floats and people in costumes.*

The French love celebrations, and all through the year there are special days when families meet to enjoy themselves.

Each religion has its own important festivals. Catholic children attend Midnight Mass on Christmas Eve, carrying candles and figures to put in the crèche. They exchange presents on Christmas Day. On Easter they hunt for chocolate eggs hidden in the house or yard. Each year they celebrate their "name day," the day honoring the saint for whom they are named.

During the Jewish festival of **Passover**, families gather to eat and pray together. During the Muslim festival of *Id ul-fitr*, people eat special foods and exchange gifts.

16

"I wear the costume of Alsace for village fêtes."

"I am Barbara, and I live in Alsace, in eastern France. Many regions of France have their own special costumes, songs and dances. Here I am wearing the costume of Alsace. I dress up like this a few times a year, for village fêtes and other celebrations."

"I will be a full member of the Jewish community after my Bar Mitzvah."

"I am Jeremie. When I am thirteen years old, I will celebrate my Bar Mitzvah. This means that I will become a full member of the Jewish community. I will read from the Jewish scriptures in the **synagogue**, then my family and friends will come to my home to celebrate with me."

On July 14 French people celebrate **Bastille Day** with parties and fireworks. People also celebrate their own regional festivals in the countryside.

Homes

In large towns and cities most people live in apartments. Often, there is a balcony where the family can sit, or hang out their laundry.

In Paris and other big cities there may be a caretaker, called a *concierge*, who keeps an eye on things from a small office near the lobby of the building. There are many tall apartment buildings but also newer developments with lower buildings.

Outside the cities are the **suburbs**. Here there are single-family houses with yards, as well as apartment buildings.

Apartment buildings can be found in many French towns and cities.

18

"Our apartment is on the eighth floor."

"I am Alexandre. I live in an apartment building in Lyons. Our apartment is on the eighth floor and we have a balcony overlooking the rooftops. My sister Anna and I each have our own room. Here I am playing cards with Anna."

"I have lots of other children to play with."

"I am Olivier, and I live in the country. On our farm there are three families living together. Dad runs the farm with my two uncles. Besides my brother and sister, I have all my cousins to play with. Here we all are together!"

In the villages some people still live in old stone cottages and farmhouses. Many of these have features that are special to the region. But some features remain the same all over France, like the shutters on the windows that are used to keep out the wind and rain.

Sports and pastimes

Soccer is very popular and enjoyed by millions of people in France. Bicycling is another favorite sport. The national bicycle race, the Tour de France, takes place every year and cyclists come from all over the world to take part. Automobile racing is also popular, and the Le Mans 24-hour race, a great auto racing event, takes place in France.

Many French families enjoy winter sports. They often vacation on the snowy slopes of the Alps or the Pyrenees.

In the summer, families enjoy vacations at the beach. They go to the beaches on the Atlantic and the Mediterranean coasts. They often take tents with them because

A game of boules played in a town square.

"I like skateboarding and watching television."

"I am Alexandre. Although we live in a city, our apartment is near a beautiful park where I go skateboarding. On weekends, we sometimes walk or go for a picnic in the country. At home, I like listening to music and watching television. Here I am watching television with Mom and my sister Anna."

"I like bicycling with my Mom and Dad and my brothers."

"My name is Sophie. My favorite pastimes are swimming, playing with my cat and riding my bicycle. Here I am with Mom and Dad and my brothers Nicholas and Cédric. We all like bicycling!"

camping is very popular in France.

Other favorite sports are canoeing, windsurfing and mountaineering. The game of *boules*, which is similar to lawn bowling, is played all over France.

Food

Market stalls often sell a wide range of fresh foods, like the cheeses on display here.

France is world famous for its delicious food. Every region has its own special dishes and ways of cooking.

People living near the coasts eat lots of fish. In the Mediterranean region they make a special fish soup using many different types of fish.

France has the largest number of different cheeses in the world. Brie, Camembert and Roquefort are all famous French cheeses.

There are also many types and shapes of bread. French people buy fresh bread every day to eat with meals. They eat flaky rolls called *croissants* for breakfast.

"I like to eat spaghetti or steak with French fries."

"My name is Ludovic. Dad runs a restaurant near Grasse. Some of the dishes on the menu are specialties from our region, like rabbit cooked with mustard or a special salad called *salade niçoise*. But my favorites are spaghetti and steak with French fries!"

"I like my father's cakes but I like fruit too."

"I am Laura. Here I am outside Dad's bakery. Dad bakes bread twice every day. He makes long white loaves called *baguettes* and lots of other kinds of bread. He also makes a special bread with nuts, and a cake with almonds. I like bread and cakes but I like fruit too, especially melons!"

Some French dishes are eaten all over the world, such as *crêpes suzette* (pancakes) and *coq au vin* (chicken cooked in red wine). One special dish is cooked snails, eaten hot with butter and garlic.

Shopping

In France there are many small stores selling only one kind of product. A *charcuterie* sells cold meats. A *patisserie* sells cakes and tarts. The *boulangerie* sells freshly-baked bread.

Many people like to shop every day for bread, fruit and vegetables. In most towns there are open-air markets. These are usually held in the town square. Often there is a market once or twice a week, and farmers and gardeners bring their produce to sell. There may also be stalls selling flowers, clothes and household goods.

Although many French people like to shop at small stores or market stalls, others

A charcuterie has all kinds of meat and sausages for sale.

do all their shopping in one place. They like to shop at a giant supermarket called a "hypermarket," where they can buy everything from food to furniture.

"Lots of vegetables grow in the south of France."

"I am Sophie. There is an open-air market twice a week in our town. Here I am shopping with Mom. The stalls sell clothes, flowers, fruit and vegetables. Many vegetables are grown here in the south of France, like green beans, peppers and eggplant."

"You can buy everything at the hypermarket."

"My name is Jean, and I live in Brittany. Once a week Mom shops at the big hypermarket just outside our town. She says it is cheaper to shop here. You can buy everything here — food, clothes, toys and things for the car. Here I am, helping Mom to put the bags in the car. There is a big parking lot near the hypermarket."

Transportation

In France, all kinds of transportation can be found, from modern subways in the big cities, to barges carrying goods by river and canal.

The main superhighways, called *autoroutes*, are all linked to the capital city, Paris. Drivers have to pay a **toll** to use the *autoroutes* but other main roads are free. Trucks carry **freight** by road all over France. Freight is also carried by rail. French railroads are efficient and very fast. The TGV trains (*Trains Grande Vitesse*) that run between Paris and other big cities are among the fastest in the world.

Autoroute drivers must stop at a booth to pay for their tickets.

"I take the school bus to the next village."

"I am Arnaud. There used to be a school in my village but it closed a few years ago. Now I take the school bus to the next village. The bus comes right to my home and drops me off at the school gates. Then in the evening it takes me and my friends from other villages home."

"I go to school by car."

"I am Sophie. Mom or Dad takes me to school every day in the car. My brother Nicholas sometimes goes to school on his bike. He's fourteen years old so he can ride a small motorbike now. My other brother Cédric is seventeen. He has a motorcycle, and he is also learning to drive a car."

In towns and cities, where there is a lot of traffic, many people use small motorbikes to get around.

Air France is the country's largest airline. It has a large fleet of aircraft including the **supersonic** airliner Concorde.

Let's discuss France

This book has told us a little about France and the French people. Now that you have read the book, what do you think about France? In what ways does it seem different from your country?

Alexandre and Arnaud have talked about their schools. Is your school different from theirs? Arnaud has just started learning English. Do you know any French words? Ludovic and Laura have told us what they like to eat. What are your favorite foods? Are they different?

Facts
Population: 56 million
Capital: Paris
Language: French
Money: French franc
Religion: Mainly Roman Catholic

The Eiffel Tower in Paris is a famous landmark.

Make a list of any goods you see around you that come from France. Perhaps a kind of cheese or a special cake came originally from France, or maybe a make of car or a kind of perfume.

Is your home in a town or in the country? How would you describe your home if you were talking to one of the children in this book? Imagine one of the children is your pen pal and tell him or her all about yourself.

The landscape near Grasse in the south of France, where many French perfumes are made.

Glossary

Bastille Day A special day, July 14, celebrated every year by French people. It commemorates the storming of the Bastille (a prison in Paris) in 1789, which began the French Revolution.

Christianity The religion based on the teachings of Jesus Christ.

Colonies Territories occupied and governed by settlers from a ruling country.

Communion An important service of the Roman Catholic and other Christian religions.

Confirmation A ceremony of the Christian Church by which people become full members of the Church.

Fashion shows Shows where models demonstrate new and exciting clothes made by fashion designers.

Freight The load or cargo carried by ships, trucks, trains etc.

Hebrew script The ancient writing of the Jewish people.

Islam The religion based on the teachings of Mohammed. People who practice this religion are called Muslims.

Mardi Gras The French name for Shrove Tuesday, the last day before Lent begins.

Multicultural Made up of many different social and religious groups.

Passover A festival celebrated by Jews every year to commemorate the time when Moses led them out of captivity.

Pastures Areas of land with grass growing on them for animals to feed on.

Region An area of land or a district.

Suburbs Districts surrounding the central area of a large town or city.

Supersonic Capable of traveling at a speed faster than sound.

Synagogue A Jewish place of worship.

Toll A tax that must be paid when using certain roads.

Tourism The industry that deals with vacationers and tourists.

Vineyard A farm where grapes are grown for making wine.

Books to read

Countries of the World, France by
    Alan Blackwood and Brigitte
    Chosson (Bookwright, 1988)
A Family in France by A.D.
    Jacobsen and P. Kristensen
    (Bookwright, 1984)

Inside France by Ian James
    (Franklin Watts, 1988)
Passport to France by Dominique
    Norbrook (Franklin Watts, 1985)
We Live in France by James
    Tomlins (Bookwright, 1983)

Picture acknowledgments

All photographs are by Julia Davey except for the following: pages 6, 16 by
Topham; front cover, pages 7 (lower) 14, 28 by Zefa. Maps on contents page
and page 5 by Jenny Hughes.

Index